UPDATE:
Gun Control

by Paul Almonte and Theresa Desmond

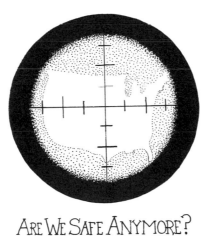

Are We Safe Anymore?

Crestwood House
Parsippany, New Jersey

Cartoon drawings by Jim Kirschman

PHOTO CREDITS
Cover: AP Wide World Photos
AP Wide World Photos: 6, 23, 28, 42
Brian Vaughan: 10, 15, 35

Published by Crestwood House, an imprint of Silver Burdett Press.
A Simon & Schuster Company
299 Jefferson Road, Parsippany, NJ 07054

First edition
Printed in the United States of America

10 9 8 7 6 5 4 3 2 1   *3103 5 0 0 6 7 3 2 9 8 5*

Library of Congress Cataloging-in-Publication Data

Almonte, Paul.
    Gun control / Paul Almonte & Theresa Desmond.
            p. cm. — (Update)
            ISBN 0-89686-809-5
            1. Gun control — United States — Juvenile literature. [1. Gun control.
    2. Firearms — Law and legislation.] I. Desmond, Theresa. II. Title.
    III. Series: Update
    HV7436.A46   1995
    363.3'3'0973 — dc20   94-18181
        Summary: Discusses the issue of gun control and gun violence in the United
States with an emphasis on the right to bear arms. Includes a listing of organizations that help get guns off the streets.

Contents

KILLINGS AND CONTROVERSY

ARE WE SAFE ANYMORE?

On August 28, 1993, two **homicides** were reported on the same page of *New York Newsday.* The story at the top of page 5 told of the death of Toya Gillard, a 17-year-old killed in Brooklyn. She had been in the courtyard of her housing project when she heard gunshots ring out. She ran to protect her 2-year-old son, but a bullet hit her in the back of the head before she could reach him. Toya died instantly, caught in the crossfire between two feuding teenagers.

At the bottom of the page was a story about Ana Ruiz, a 60-year-old woman. Ruiz was shot as she walked home from evening prayers at the East Harlem church where she worked and worshiped. Bullets had hit her in the shoulder and in the head. Police believe she was killed by a 15-year-old who was firing a .25 caliber handgun through a window for kicks. He was thought to be under the influence of the drug angel dust.

Two women, two "accidental" shootings, two deaths.

Did You Know...?

• In July 1992, *The New Yorker* Magazine reported that an American Medical Association study found that "firearm homicide" was the second leading cause of death among teenagers. Homicides by firearms had risen 23 percent in three years among high schoolers in the suburbs, and 28 percent in the inner cities.

• The January 1993 issue of the *Atlantic Monthly* quoted statistics from the Department of Justice showing that "every twenty-four hours handgun wielding assailants rape thirty-three women, rob 575 people, and assault another 1,116."

A young woman buys two nightsticks in response to killings in her Florida college community.

When stories like these are reported, a public outcry follows. Aren't we safe anywhere? Must we hide in our homes? Why do teenagers have guns? And how can such violence happen so casually?

But when it comes to knowing how to stop such incidents, Americans seem unable to agree on a solution. What we need, many people say, is stricter gun control. After all, it is estimated that there are over 200 million firearms in the United States today. But other people say that guns aren't the problem—it's the people who use them. And still other people think it's not just guns or people that are to blame. Rather it's the combination of the two in a society where violence is commonplace and even glamourized. There wouldn't be so much violence if guns weren't so readily available. And there wouldn't be such a scramble for guns if violence wasn't accepted and even encouraged. Will controlling the availability of guns help curb violence?

Many Americans seem to think that it would. A recent **Harris Poll** found that "more than four in five adults surveyed felt that the easy availability of guns and the sheer number of weapons contributed to an atmosphere of violence that endangered children." Still, people respond differently to that atmosphere of violence. While some believe it can be lessened only by restricting access to guns, others say we must have more guns to defend ourselves from the growing violence.

The issue of gun control is not simply an argument between the **National Rifle Association**—which **lobbies** against most gun control legislation—and those who would forbid the sale of most guns to most people. Most people's views lie somewhere between these two positions. In a *Time* magazine survey, 92 percent of those polled favored a five day waiting period for anyone who wants to buy a gun. Sixty-five percent said stricter gun control laws are needed. The question of gun control, then, may be: How much control would be effective, and what form should that control take?

The term *gun control* doesn't refer only to restrictions on those who want to keep loaded handguns in their night-stands or hunting rifles in their cars. It covers many issues: how guns are obtained illegally; when people have the right to use guns; how to keep guns away from those who are not capable of using them properly; how guns contribute to rising crime rates and youth crime; how guns are related to an atmosphere of violence in our country.

The Second Amendment
Whenever gun control is discussed, the **Second Amendment** to the United States Constitution is likely to be brought up. The amendment states: "A well regulated militia, being necessary to the security of a free State, the right of the people to keep and bear arms, shall not be infringed." Many people interpret the amendment to mean that Americans have a constitutional right to own guns ("keep and bear arms"). To them, it seems as basic as the right to a fair trial.

But this isn't the only interpretation of the Second Amendment. Some say that the amendment's original intent

The History of the NRA

The National Rifle Association was started in 1871 in New York City. Back then, it was a small group of people who got together to practice **marksmanship**, or target shooting. Today, its 3.2 million members include such influential people as former presidents Ronald Reagan and George Bush, and movie legend Charlton Heston.

Today, the NRA spends much of its time and money arguing against gun control and lobbying to keep "the right to bear arms" free from government interference. Gun control, the NRA argues, does not get at the root of crime. The group feels that instead of "criminalizing" law-abiding citizens who keep guns for hunting or self-defense, government should be tougher on crime by handing out longer prison sentences.

Gun magazines try to appeal to young people who want to be tough.

was to create a "well regulated militia." When the amendment was written, in colonial times, many private citizens were also members of local armies or militias. They kept guns at home in case their brigade was suddenly called into service. Today, we no longer serve in local armies, and some people argue that the amendment has only historic meaning. They feel strongly that it shouldn't be interpreted to mean that citizens can keep guns for self-defense or as part of a collection.

However, the Supreme Court has ruled that citizens may own guns, but it has also said that laws controlling guns are constitutional. Congress *can* make laws that restrict the use of guns without violating the Second Amendment. But what kind of laws will reduce gun-related violence without penalizing gun owners who use their weapons responsibly?

Yoshihiro Hattori

In October 1992, Yoshihiro Hattori, a 16-year-old Japanese exchange student, and a friend were on their way to a Halloween party at a private home in Louisiana. Hattori and his friend mistakenly rang the doorbell of the wrong house.

Bonnie Peairs answered her doorbell and saw a stranger standing there. She told her husband to get his gun. He did. Mr. Peairs yelled, "Freeze!" at Hattori. But the exchange student's English wasn't very good, and he kept moving. So Mr. Peairs shot him in the chest, killing him.

The incident sparked both national and international concern because of the questions it raised about guns, violence, and fear. How could a young man be shot for an innocent mistake? Mr. Peairs was tried for killing Yoshihiro Hattori, but a jury felt that his actions were justified and found him not guilty. Because he had felt threatened in his own home, the jury decided, he was legally justified in using lethal force.

The verdict caused an uproar. Legal experts debated the circumstances of the case and the differing laws around the country. What is considered a threatening situation? Is the level of threat different when it occurs in someone's home?

Others argued about the use of a gun in this case. Mr. Peairs's lawyer said, "In your house, if you want to do it, you have the legal right to answer everybody that comes to your door with a gun." Some experts agreed, saying a gun is often an effective deterrent to crime. Gary Kleck, a professor of criminal justice and criminology at Florida State University, said that many times "the presence of a gun, without a shot being fired, wards off a criminal action."

But individuals and organizations like Handgun Control worry that Americans now think that they can take the law into their own hands. And coupled with a fear of crime, this "vigilante" attitude can lead to the killing of innocent people like Yoshihiro Hattori. As a Handgun Control spokeswoman says, "Guns don't make us safer, they just escalate the violence."

Basically, there are two ways to get guns: legally and illegally. The success of any gun control program depends on monitoring the system by which guns are bought legally as well as on preventing illegal access to guns. To do both of those things, authorities have tried to check on the background of those wanting to buy guns, and have attempted to restrict the movement of guns from one state, county, or other locality to another. But such measures have not only met with opposition, they are also often ineffective.

To obtain a gun from a licensed dealer, a buyer has to fill out a form and pay a $30 licensing fee. Form 4473 asks the buyer if he or she is a drug addict, mentally ill, or a convicted felon, among other things. Of course, the buyer can simply lie, and the dealer can't really check on the answers. The only time the answers are checked is when the gun is used in a crime—that is, *after* a crime has been committed. Under

Did You Know...?

• In July 1992, *The New Yorker* noted that "the huge majority of gunshot deaths and injuries are inflicted not by career criminals using illegal weapons but by ordinary citizens."

• According to the *New York Times*, firearms kill 65 Americans every day.

• The *New Yorker* reported that "the firearm-homicide rate in the United States is nearly seven times that of Australia, fifty-five times that of Britain, and fifty-eight times that of Japan."

federal law, a buyer must also show that he or she is at least 21 and lives in the state where the dealer is located.

The Gun Control Act of 1968 made it illegal for gun dealers nationwide to sell firearms to out-of-state residents. It was hoped that this law might cut down on the flow of weapons from one state to another. For example, the gun used by Lee Harvey Oswald to assassinate President John F. Kennedy in 1963 was purchased by mail order. The rifle was simply sent through the mail from Chicago to Texas. The Gun Control Act was intended to stop sales like this.

But in 1986 another federal law was passed, the Firearms Owners Protection Act. This law—lobbied for by the National Rifle Association—made it easier to buy, sell, and transport guns across state lines. At the federal level, then, there is little regulation of gun purchases. That's one reason why states like Virginia have become the centers of a growing gun trade. Virginia has relatively lax gun laws, and its central location on the eastern seaboard means that guns purchased in Virginia can be easily transported to northeastern states.

Virginia's governor has proposed stricter state gun laws, and other states and cities are also making new laws about acquiring guns. For example, the Chicago suburb of Morton Grove has made it illegal to sell or possess any handgun in that town. In 1987 the state of Florida passed a law making it legal to carry a concealed handgun in public. Florida lawmakers were responding to the same high crime rates that

Gun violence is on the rise all over the United States, but urban areas have the highest number of shooting deaths.

concerned the citizens of Morton Grove, but in a very different way than the Illinois town did.

But as a November 1991 article in *Scientific American* pointed out, the sheer number of guns in a state is related to the gun crime rate. "The percentage of gun-related crimes in an area is related to the proportion of owners of firearms in that area," the article said. When there are more guns available for everyone, there are more guns available for crime. A 1992 article in the *New Yorker* compared the cities of Seattle and Vancouver, Washington. In Seattle, there are few restrictions on buying guns. In Vancouver, potential gun buyers must get a special permit, and they cannot buy a gun simply for self-defense. Seattle's homicide rate is 65 percent higher than Vancouver's.

Despite the restrictions on the legal purchase and possession of guns, many guns are still acquired illegally. Most guns used in crimes were not bought from licensed gun dealers. Some were stolen, borrowed from friends, or purchased on the street through the **black market**. In the end, laws regulating gun shops and dealers may have no effect on the availability of a gun for someone willing to obtain it illegally. As a *Time* magazine story on "Doug," a teenager in Omaha, showed, this 16-year-old had no trouble buying a gun. A classmate introduced Doug to an illegal dealer who sold Doug a shotgun from the trunk of his car for a mere $25.

The ease with which teenagers can get guns continues to be a problem. Lawmakers in many states are trying to toughen the laws to make it harder for teens to buy guns. In Colorado, Governor Roy Romer signed a bill that makes it illegal for people under the age of 18 to have guns, except those used for hunting. The law also makes it a felony for any adult to purchase guns for a minor. The governor is hoping that this law will help reduce the teenage crime rate, which has risen in Colorado over the past few years. Colorado is now one of 18 states where it is illegal for teenagers to own handguns.

Gun Violence

Of course, having a gun doesn't necessarily mean you're going to commit a crime. But the presence of guns in society seems to aid in the overall commis-

Super Soaker

In June 1992, 16-year-old Richard Cook of New York was shot in the back with a 9-millimeter gun. Why? It wasn't a random shooting. It wasn't a gang battle. It wasn't a drug buy. Richard had just squirted someone with his Super Soaker, a giant water gun. That person got angry and he shot Richard. Earlier that summer, a 15-year-old in Boston was killed for the same reason.

Public officials were angered when they heard about the senseless shootings, so they called for stricter gun control. The catch? The guns they wanted to regulate or ban weren't the real guns but the squirt guns!

sion of crimes. In his book *Violent Crime and Gun Control*, Gerald Robin reported that guns are used in over 60 percent of murders, 10 percent of rapes, 23 percent of aggravated assaults, and over 40 percent of robberies. If there weren't so many guns, would there be as much crime?

Some sociologists say no. They say that the mere availability of guns may lead to more violent behavior. In other words, behavior changes when guns are around. A person may not have intended to cause harm or commit a crime but may do so when there is access to a gun. For example, in the heat of a family argument, when family members are angry and emotional, someone may grab a nearby gun. But if there is no gun around, the person would have to find another way of dealing with the anger. Perhaps the person wouldn't even think of using a gun.

In one study, social psychologists found that the very presence of guns seemed to make children more aggressive. Four- and five-year-olds were given different toys to play with. The children playing with toy guns were more likely to display antisocial behavior, like hitting and pushing, than the children who were playing with other toys.

Some people argue that a criminal is going to reach for a weapon no matter what the situation. Even if a gun isn't around, a person who really wants to commit a crime will find a weapon. Still, the type of weapon used can make an enormous difference. An assault with a gun is five times more likely to cause death than an assault with a knife. And "in cases where robberies result in injuries, guns are far more deadly than other weapons." So even when someone does think about using a weapon, the kind of weapon that is available affects the level of harm that can be caused.

Police Firepower

With criminals packing more powerful and dangerous weapons, police departments have responded by arming their officers with even more firepower. But some people feel that if police officers are given stronger weapons like semiautomatics, it will only lead to an increase in violence and accidents. Other people disagree. They feel that the police should have firepower equal to what the criminals use.

In New York City, the police department is training its officers to use 9-millimeter semiautomatic weapons. One officer told *New York Newsday* that the police need faster guns "so we can at least meet the criminals head on." Some examples suggest that police officers without semiautomatic weapons are being outgunned by criminals. When officer Richard DeGaetano was shot, he barely escaped with his life. The gunman had fired 28 times from three guns. As horrible as it was, DeGaetano said getting shot between the eyes was one of the luckiest breaks of his life. "If I had made it up the stairs and had to face a guy carrying three automatics, I'd be Swiss cheese now."

One of the most talked about gun control measures in recent years was the Brady Act, which was passed in early 1994. The bill was named for James Brady, the former White House press secretary to President Ronald Reagan. Brady was shot and permanently disabled when John Hinckley, Jr., attempted to assassinate then President Reagan in 1981. Brady and his wife, Sarah, launched a lobbying campaign for stronger gun control measures.

Their proposal, known as the Brady bill, called for a mandatory waiting period for handgun purchases. The waiting period can be both a cooling off and a checking out period. People in a stressed out state would not be able to buy—or use—a gun. At the same time, local authorities could use the time to run a background check on potential buyers.

The Brady bill was a limited measure. It did not address the problem of guns that were already in the hands of crimi-

Did You Know...?

• According to the National Center for Health Statistics, gunshots cause 1 of every 4 deaths. In 1985, 2,500 teenagers were killed by bullets; in 1990, it was 4,200 teenagers. And according to the National Education Association, 100,000 students carry a gun to school.

• A U.S. Health and Human Services Department report said that black men aged 15 to 24 were ten times more likely to die from homicides than white males of the same ages. Between 1985 and 1990, gunshot deaths for black males between 15 and 24 years old more than doubled.

nals or mentally unstable people. And it did not *require* police to check those who want to buy a handgun.

The Brady bill was defeated by Congress when it was proposed in 1988. But three years later the bill received support from former President Reagan, himself a member of the National Rifle Association. By 1993, the bill had steadily gained public support. As *U.S. News & World Report* noted in March 1993, "88 percent of gun owners support the Brady Bill and 60 percent favor a total ban on assault weapons." With so many Americans calling for ways to reduce crime and with President Clinton's support, the bill was passed by both houses of Congress. The Brady Act took effect on February 28, 1994.

The waiting period called for by the Brady Act is only one method of gun control. The American Medical Association has proposed a plan of gun registration and licensing. It suggests that guns should be licensed just as cars are, and that gun users should have to show ability, just as drivers do. The plan would require gun owners to be of a certain age, show knowledge of proper firearm use, and have their performance monitored at regular intervals.

But waiting periods and registration plans are only preventive methods. They don't solve the problem of guns that are obtained illegally or that are already on the streets. Some cities feel that they have to tackle these gun problems right away, before preventive measures can be effective. Some cities have tried buy-back programs, where they offer to purchase guns from anyone who wants to turn one in—no questions asked. City officials simply give each person a flat fee for each gun brought to them. Officials have been surprised by the number of guns buy back programs produce.

Buy back plans got a huge boost in December 1993, when anti-gun activist Fernando Mateo organized a "Gifts for Guns" trade-in program in New York City. With the help of police and a toy store chain, Mateo offered people $100 gift certificates if they handed in a gun. In this drive alone, over 1,500 guns were collected.

Mateo's idea was so successful that similar programs popped up across the country. In Paterson, New Jersey, a "Food for Guns" program was started. In Jacksonsville, Florida, people who traded in guns received $25 and a chance to win tickets to the Super Bowl. Other states now give toys,

A Miami police detective in street clothes records handguns turned in during a state buy-back program.

food, beds, and even Bibles in exchange for guns. Thousands of guns are being turned in nationwide. And to expand gun trade-in efforts, New York Representative Charles Schumer plans to introduce legislation that will give tax breaks to companies that contribute goods to gun trade-in programs.

States Take Steps
Because states, cities, and towns make their own policies regarding gun control, the debate has taken different forms in different locales. A sampling:

Chicago

Chicago's housing projects have been especially hard hit by gun violence. In 1991, one person was killed every month in the projects. Every week there was one new gunshot victim and a new report of an innocent bystander being shot at.

The Housing Authority of Chicago knew something had to be done. It began to enforce an old rule that tenants could not keep guns on the grounds of the projects. Hundreds of weapons were taken away.

But the National Rifle Association objected to the weapons ban. Representatives from the NRA said that the rule was a violation of the Second Amendment. Residents couldn't be forced *not* to own guns, especially in the projects, they said. Since the projects had such a high crime rate, the NRA felt, residents should be able to own guns for self-defense.

Even if guns were permitted in the projects, do project residents really want them? Eighty percent of them are sin-

Colin Ferguson opened fire on a Long Island Railroad commuter train in December 1993, killing six people and wounding nineteen.

APP[
FINGE[

gle mothers on welfare. As one member of a Mothers' Guild group at one of the projects said, "I was raised in Mississippi, and my father had guns around the house. But he always [said] that guns are not for killing humans."

In addition, the NRA claimed that the gun ban was racially discriminatory since most of the project residents are black. But some find it hypocritical for the NRA to bring up the subject of race at all. They point out that the NRA didn't mention that almost all the victims of the gun violence are black. In fact, young black males suffer by far the highest rate of **homicide** from firearms of any group in America. As the chief of the housing police said of the NRA, "They have never cared about black people before."

In October 1991, 35-year-old George Hennard drove his pickup truck through the front window of Luby's Cafeteria in Killeen, Texas. He jumped from the truck into the crowded cafeteria at the height of the lunchtime rush. Yelling, "This is what Bell County did to me. This is payback day!" he began firing his two semiautomatic pistols, shooting bullets in every direction. In ten minutes, he had killed 23 people. He then shot himself in the head. It was the worst mass murder in our country's history.

Two years earlier, 24-year-old Patrick Purdy had walked up to an elementary school playground in Stockton, California. Nearly 450 school children were at recess. Purdy held up his AK47 rifle and began firing. He fired 100 rounds in two minutes, killing five children and wounding 29 others. Purdy's last shot was a bullet to his head.

The mass killings in Killeen and Stockton made national headlines. People reacted with horror. How could two obviously disturbed men get guns? Was there any way their actions could have been prevented?

When he purchased his gun, Purdy had used a false name. Hennard had been thrown out of the merchant marine for drug possession, and this had left him depressed. But, despite his unstable past, he was still able to purchase a gun.

In December 1993, another mass killing focused attention on the gun control debate. A man named Colin Ferguson pulled out a 9-millimeter semiautomatic gun on a commuter train in Long Island, New York, and randomly opened fire on the passengers. Before he was tackled by three men while reloading his weapon, Ferguson had killed 6 and wounded 19 others. Ferguson, an African American, had left strange notes saying he was out to get whites and Asians. He also denounced some African American leaders. People thought he was crazy. How could such a man get a gun?

Ferguson had purchased his gun legally. He had moved to California, living in a motel to establish residency there. He went to a gun store and put down a deposit on a 9-millimeter Ruger. After the waiting period for purchasing a gun was over, he went to the shop and picked up his weapon. Then, on that train in December, he opened fire.

After the Texas killing, a measure was brought before Congress to ban certain assault weapons and ammunition clips, but the measure was defeated. Public outcry simply could not outweigh the National Rifle Association's lobbying strength.

Nevertheless, these three atrocities brought the arguments about gun control to a new pitch. The NRA's familiar slogans—"Guns don't kill people, people kill people" and "If guns are criminal, only criminals will have guns"—no longer seemed to ring true. The easy access that Hennard, Purdy, and Ferguson had to destructive weapons made their crazed actions possible. Even former Los Angeles Police Chief Daryl Gates stated: "There is no need for citizens to have highly sophisticated military assault rifles designed for the sole purpose of killing people on the battlefield."

Texas

In 1993, two pieces of proposed legislation set off heated debate in Texas. One bill would ban *assault rifles* statewide. The other would allow residents to obtain permits to carry concealed weapons in public. Two proposals, two very different ideas—and both in the same state.

In Texas, four out of ten people own more than two guns. According to the Texas Rifle Association, there are 68 million guns in the state. That's almost four guns for every person in the state.

The unusual number of guns in Texas may be partly due to what one gun shop owner calls "tradition." Leo Bradshaw, who owns Used Guns and Other Keen Stuff, says, "Texans enjoy their guns and owning them. It's a way of life. It's the way people were brought up here."

Still, many Texans favor a law that bans assault rifles. According to one poll, a majority of gun owners themselves approve of an assault rifle ban. And 90 percent of them favor a mandatory waiting period to buy the rifles. Nevertheless, some Texas lawmakers worry that an assault rifle ban might cost them votes when they come up for re-election.

But the other bill, which would let people obtain **carry permits** to carry concealed weapons, seems to have more support among legislators. The lawmaker who sponsored the bill says that the people in his district want to protect themselves. But as others have pointed out, that kind of protection means trying to stop gun violence with more guns. Carrying hidden weapons, they say, seems like a dangerous way to decrease the damage weapons have already caused. A poll released by the Texas Police Chiefs Association said that "70 percent of Texans opposed the legislation."

New Jersey

In New Jersey, the political battle over gun control has been even more intense than in Texas. New Jersey has some of the toughest gun control laws in the country. Most semi-automatic assault weapons are banned, and former Governor Jim Florio was a strong supporter of strict regulations for owning a gun.

That didn't make Florio a favorite of the National Rifle Association. The group even launched a campaign to prevent Florio's re-election in 1993. It paid for television and radio announcements and backed candidates whose views on gun control were similar to theirs. A lobbyist for the NRA says its response to Florio wasn't about politics. It was simply about the effectiveness of the gun ban. Richard Manning said, "I've got 300,000 people who have been turned into felons in this state because of a law that is ineffective and doing nothing about crime."

But, while lawmakers and lobbyists argue about control and money, the citizens' voices aren't being heard. Polls have shown that a large majority of New Jersey residents are in favor of the gun ban.

Wilbert Rideau

Wilbert Rideau is a 51-year-old prisoner at Louisiana State Penitentiary at Angola. He's been there since 1962, serving a life sentence for murder. Rideau has spent part of that time becoming a writer and a prison reform advocate—and he's had a lot of time to think about gun control.

Rideau thinks that a good education is the best deterrent to crime. But what would have deterred him?

"I've thought a lot about that," he said in an interview with _Time_ magazine in 1993. "I know that if I hadn't been able to walk into a pawnshop and buy a handgun as easily as I did, I wouldn't have robbed that bank. That applies to just about everybody in this prison who ever held up anybody. Nobody robs a place with a knife or a can of Mace. I was 19, an eighth grade dropout. If I'd known that things weren't as helpless as I thought they were, that would have stopped me. I wouldn't have felt so frustrated."

WHO'S RESPONSIBLE?

I t's clear that gun violence is a problem in the United States. But whose fault is it? Who should take the blame?

Dealers and Manufacturers   When someone is arrested for drug possession, law enforcement officials usually want to know who sold that person the drugs. They want the seller—and, hopefully, the supplier—of the drugs to be held responsible for the illegal sale.

When a gun is used in a crime, the seller and the supplier are rarely held liable for the crime. Unlike drugs, guns are legal, and many gun manufacturers and dealers follow the

Did You Know...?

• A Harris Poll that questioned 10- to 19-year-olds found that 9 percent of them said they had fired a gun at someone, and 11 percent had been shot at. Forty percent said they knew someone who had been killed or wounded by gunfire. Sixty percent said they could get a handgun, and 15 percent said they had carried a handgun during the past month.

• Juvenile arrests for weapons violations increased 62 percent between 1987 and 1991. In 1991, one out of five arrests for weapons violations was a juvenile arrest.

• A study of Seattle high school students showed that 34 percent had ready access to handguns; 11.4 percent of all boys owned a gun; 6.6 percent of boys had carried a gun to school.

Another study reports that "645,000 high school students—one out of every 20—have carried a gun to school at least once."

law closely. A manufacturer can't make certain types of guns; a dealer must be licensed and keep the proper forms; the buyer has to be 21. Even if every manufacturer and dealer follow the rules exactly, guns can still get into the wrong hands. Some observers believe that more of the people involved in a gun transaction should be concerned about what happens to the gun once it's left their hands.

For example, the dealer in a gun shop may sell a gun to a customer who seems strange or disturbed. If the customer is 21, fills out the form properly and has the money, and the dealer fulfills all legal requirements, then the sale can go through.

But should the dealer sell a gun to someone whose character seems questionable? One gun shop owner said he doesn't want the responsibility of judging every buyer's potential for harm. "I just would not want to put myself in the position of deciding someone else's character arbitrarily, based on my own opinion," said the gun dealer.

But others argue that people who profit from the sale of guns should also bear part of the blame when guns are misused. They say that manufacturers and dealers should go beyond following the minimum regulations. As one Baltimore police officer said, "The premise seems to be that if they've got the right to do something, then that's the right thing to do." But just because an act is legal doesn't mean it's the responsible or fair thing to do.

A 1993 court case in Florida focused attention on responsibility for guns and killings. A jury in Tampa ordered Kmart

David Kenney was only 12 years old when he was accidentally killed by his 11-year-old friend. The two boys were playing with a loaded gun when a bullet discharged and struck David. The gun belonged to the friend's father, a part-time police officer.

David's mother, Susan, was grief-stricken after the accident. But Susan did more than mourn. She started a group called GRIEF—Gun Responsibility in Every Family. This group lobbies legislatures to pass laws that would make an adult **liable** in a shooting that causes injury or death if the adult left a loaded gun where it was "easily accessible" to someone 16 or younger. Such a law would create a penalty of up to five years in prison and a $5,000 fine. In Susan Kenney's home state of Connecticut, the law was passed in 1991.

Kenney feels that such a law could have prevented the accidental shooting that killed her son. If adults know that they will be held responsible for their weapons and can be punished if those weapons become available to children, then they might be more careful about storing guns.

But not everyone agrees that laws can prevent accidental shootings. The National Rifle Association, along with the Coalition of Connecticut Sportsmen, believes that you can't legislate responsibility. The legislative liaison of the NRA, James Milner, argues, "More children die each year due to accidental drowning than from the accidental discharge of firearms. Are you going to lock up all those people [their parents], too?"

Still, one Connecticut prosecutor says that any law that tries to make people responsible for gun use is a step in the right direction. As the prosecutor Eva Lenczewski says, "It's certainly better than not having any law at all."

Corporation to pay $11 million in damages to a woman who was shot with a gun purchased in one of its stores. Lawyers for the woman argued that Kmart sold the gun to the killer, the victim's boyfriend, while he was drunk. The salesperson should not have sold him the gun in his condition, they argued. And so, when he shot her, Kmart was partially responsible. The jury agreed. Gun control advocates hope that this case will make gun sellers more responsible and watchful.

Gun dealers aren't the only ones feeling the heat from the nation's outrage over gun violence. Gun and bullet manufacturers are under pressure to stop producing their most deadly products. The Winchester company, a long-time manufacturer of guns and gun products, agreed to stop producing a bullet called the **Black Talon**. The Black Talon is just one brand name of a new, more dangerous bullet that has hit the streets. Black Talons expand and split into several pieces as they hit their targets. When they enter the victim's body, these bullets cause more damage than traditional bullets. As one doctor put it, "A lone Black Talon chews up every organ it comes in contact with." Lawmakers like Representative Charles Schumer of New York have called for an outright ban on this type of bullet since it serves no reasonable purpose. Senator Daniel Patrick Moynihan, also of New York, has suggested that a high tax be placed on Black Talons, making them unaffordable to petty street criminals. Public support for the Black Talon ban persuaded the manufacturers to sell them only to law enforcement officials.

Many people believe that the media's glamorization of violence is partially responsible for the high rate of gun-related crime today.

The Role of the Media

We've all seen the images: Clint Eastwood as Dirty Harry aiming his .44 *revolver* at some "punks"; Sylvester Stallone as Rambo, ammunition slung across his chest, a machine gun in his hands. Images of gun-related violence are now commonplace in movies, television, and magazines. How do these images contribute to our attitudes about guns?

Guns have been glamourized by the media, made to look powerful but clean, and capable of giving anyone the upper hand in a macho war of right and wrong. As one writer pointed out, "The MTV mentality of *Miami Vice*—short takes, rock music, and a flimsy plot line wrapped in fleshy thighs—did as much for assault weapons as it did for razor stubble. Guns were sexy." The *Atlantic Monthly* adds, "They [movies and TV shows] teach a uniquely American lesson: When a real man has a problem, he gets his gun. He slaps in a clip, he squints grimly into the hot noon sun, and then he does what he's gotta do."

The line between fantasy and reality can get blurred. This romantic view of the hip loner out to get justice becomes so commonplace that it gets to be acceptable. Psychiatrists believe that when violent images are repeated often enough, we gradually become accustomed to them. If someone has a phobia—fear of heights, for example—a psychiatrist might gradually expose the person to what scares him or her. As time goes by the fear decreases. In the same way, we may be afraid of guns and violence, but as we're exposed to more and more images of them, we become used to them and no longer feel afraid or repulsed. Instead, they become an everyday object, even something to be admired.

As *Newsweek* noted, "Our national icons [heros] tend to be men who excel at violence, from John Wayne to Clint Eastwood." The magazine explained how the movie image was transformed into reality in 1991. Former President Bush became a national hero when he ordered bombs and missiles to be fired on Iraq during the Gulf War. At least 100,000 Iraqi civilians were killed by American firepower. It's not simply that we approve of a president's policies—we respond emotionally to the idea of one man striking out with deadly force.

Gun magazines and manufacturers recognize our attachment to images of heroism and power. Manufacturers advertise with slogans like, "As American as God, Mom, and apple pie." They give their products snappy military names like the Street Sweeper. Gun magazines run exciting stories of police shootouts and conduct consumer tests of guns and ammunition, labeling the winners the Ultimate Manstoppers!

People who sell and advertise guns, and even actors who portray criminals using guns, say that people who commit violent acts are already of a violent mind-set. An image or a phrase, they say, does not make a person into a criminal. Someone whose behavior is often violent may misinterpret messages in movies, TV, and other media. Such a person may think that because violence is okay on a TV police drama, it's okay in real life too. The average person should be able to separate fantasy from reality.

Recognizing the persuasive power the media have over people, gun control advocates have begun using advertising to get their message heard. Perhaps the most visible example of this is the new "deathclock" billboard on display in New York City. The deathclock, paid for by businessman Robert Brennan, displays the number of guns currently available across the country, as well as the estimated number of killings attributed to guns in the current year. Brennan

Paula Clouse

One afternoon in August of 1993, Paula Clouse and her 15-year-old son went to see a movie in Kansas City, Missouri. As they sat in the darkened movie theater, Paula's son suddenly pulled out a handgun and shot his mother four times in the head. Then he casually walked out of the theater into the mall, leaving his dead mother behind.

Shocked onlookers and the police immediately wondered what could have led Paula Clouse's son to commit such a violent act. The police speculated that the teenager was angry and hurt over his parents' bitter divorce. The teenager was living with his father, who owned the gun the boy used to shoot his mother.

But as the police sifted through the family's background to determine the cause of the shooting, they realized that there was really no adequate explanation. As the police captain said, "Disputes used to be settled with a shouting match or a punch in the nose." If that had been the case, perhaps no one would have heard of Paula Clouse. Now she is only one of many names on a growing list of shooting victims.

funded the project in memory of his brother, who was shot in a robbery 25 years ago. The billboard also displays a telephone number for Gun Fighters of America, a lobby and information group dedicated to gun control legislation. People who call the number will get information on gun control and can find out what position their elected representatives have taken on the issue.

THE CLINTON CRIME PACKAGE

In August 1993, President Clinton spoke to the nation about a new crime bill he was supporting. Earlier that week, the country learned that basketball star Michael Jordan's father had been found shot to death in South Carolina. As yet another victim of handgun violence was buried, people were ready to listen to the President's proposals to stop the crime epidemic.

Clinton's plan focused directly on gun control. First, it included the Brady bill, which requires a waiting period for buying a gun (as noted earlier, the Brady bill was passed into law in 1994). Then the President used his executive order power to ban the import of assault weapons (in May of 1994, Congress backed up the President by passing their own ban on assualt weapons). He proposed to make it tougher for gun dealers to get licenses by subjecting would-be dealers to background checks and fingerprinting. In some states, background checks have proven helpful in stopping some criminals from legally purchasing a weapon. Since 1989, background checks in four states—Maryland, Virginia, California, and Florida—have blocked the sale of over 47,000 guns.

The President also spoke about gun control in September 1993. As he unveiled his new health care package, Clinton said that one reason why health care is so expensive is that we have to pay for treatment for victims of gun violence. If there were tighter gun control laws, the President reasoned, there might be less gun-related violence—and less money would have to be spent on caring for the injured.

President Clinton's attorney general, Janet Reno, also favors stricter gun control measures. "The NRA doesn't particularly care for me," she told *Time* magazine. "But it's important for the NRA to understand what this stuff has done to America. I just think the American people are sick and fed up with what assault weapons have done. I can remember the first

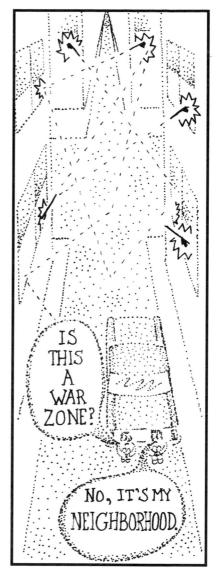

A fourteen-year-old boy checks out a 44 Magnum pistol at the National Rifle Association convention in Anaheim, California.

time I saw an assault weapon. It is deadly. It is a horrible thing. The American people have come to realize what these weapons are doing on our streets. They are saying, enough is enough."

In January 1994, the Clinton administration offered more specific proposals on how it would make it hard for gun sellers to get a license. The first idea, unveiled by Treasury Secretary Lloyd Bentsen, whose department directs the Bureau of Alcohol, Tobacco, and Firearms (ATF), was to raise the cost of a gun dealer's annual license to $600. Currently it's so inexpensive and easy to become a gun dealer that over

244,000 people have licenses. With so many people able to purchase guns at wholesale prices, gun control advocates worry that guns will remain easy to get. By making it less financially attractive to be a gun seller, the ATF estimates that 80 percent of dealers would not renew their licenses.

Besides gun control, the Clinton crime bill calls for better police protection and tougher penalties for offenders. During a five-year period, 50,000 new police officers would be put on the streets at a cost of $3.4 billion. **Boot camps** would be set up for young, first-time offenders, and the death penalty would become the punishment for 47 specific crimes.

In the summer of 1994, and after much public debate, the Congress and Senate passed the Crime Package President Clinton had pushed for. This bill provides for over $30 billion dollars to be spent on various crime prevention and enforcement programs. Some of the money will go to cities and states to hire 100,000 more police officers and build more prisons. Other money will go to programs like midnight basketball leagues that hope to steer kids away from the violent streets and into more productive places like schools and gyms. The crime bill also bans the sale and possession of 19 types of assault weapons.

The Clinton Administration is also proud of what they call "the most important" part of the Crime Package: the ban on juvenile possession of handguns. "Except when hunting or target shooting with a parent or other responsible adult, young people simply shouldn't be carrying guns, period," President Clinton said. "This provision is critical to our ability to make our schools and neighborhoods safer."

Gun Terminology

Assault rifles (like the Uzi submachine gun or the AK47) are usually about 3 feet long (unless they have folding capacity) and are semiautomatic but can be converted to automatic.

Machine guns fire rifle caliber bullets.

Submachine guns fire pistol caliber bullets.

Revolvers usually fire six rounds from a cylinder that rotates with each pull. These guns are slower than semiautomatics. "Nines" are revolvers that use 9-millimeter cartridges.

Semiautomatic weapons fire one round for every pull of the trigger.

Fully automatic weapons will keep firing as long as you pull the trigger.

FOR MORE
INFORMATION

For more information on gun control, you can write to:

Center to Prevent Handgun Violence
1225 Eye Street, NW
Suite 1150
Washington, D.C. 20005

National Rifle Association
1600 Rhode Island Avenue, NW
Washington, D.C. 20036

Handgun Control, Inc.
1225 Eye Street, NW
Suite 1100
Washington, D.C. 20005

GLOSSARY/ INDEX

BLACK MARKET—*16*   The illegal trade in legal and illegal products.

BLACK TALON—*34*   A type of bullet that expands and splits when it hits a target, causing more extensive damage than regular bullets.

BOOT CAMPS—*43*   Marine-style programs to teach discipline and possibly deter first-time offenders from criminal activity by showing them how tough life can be in prison.

BRADY ACT/BILL—*21*   A law named after President Reagan's press secretary who was maimed for life when shot with a handgun. The law provides a waiting period for the purchase of a handgun.

CARRY PERMITS—*27*   Licenses that allow people to carry concealed weapons to protect themselves.

HARRIS POLL—*7*   The Harris company, like other polling groups, asks peoples' opinions on particular topics, and then reports these findings to give a people a sense of what the nation as a whole believes.

HOMICIDE—*25*   The killing of any human being by another.

LIABLE—*33*   Being legally obligated or responsible for the consequences of an action

LOBBYING—*7*   To try to influence politicians to vote a certain way

MARKSMANSHIP—*9*   The ability to shoot guns accurately

NATIONAL RIFLE ASSOCIATION (NRA)—*7*   An organization that lobbies governments and politicians in order to protect the rights of gun owners and users.

SECOND AMENDMENT (TO THE U.S. CONSTITU-TION)—*8*   An amendment that states "A well-regulated militia, being necessary to the security of a free State, the right of the people to keep and bear arms shall not be infringed."